ALL ABOUT
Coding Statements

BY JACLYN JAYCOX

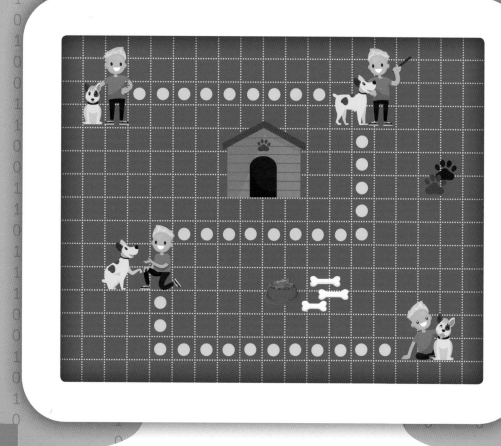

The Child's World®
childsworld.com

Published by The Child's World®
1980 Lookout Drive • Mankato, MN 56003-1705
800-599-READ • www.childsworld.com

Photographs ©: Shutterstock Images, cover (boy with dog), 1 (boy with dog), 4, 6, 16, 24; Anuta Berg/Shutterstock Images, cover (dog house), cover (paw prints), cover (bones), 1 (dog house), 1 (paw prints), 1 (bones); iStockphoto, 5; Koldunova Anna/Shutterstock Images, 9; Natasa Adzic/Shutterstock Images, 10; Bulltus Casso/Shutterstock Images, 15; ESB Professional/Shutterstock Images, 18

ISBN 9781503832008
LCCN 2018962884

Printed in the United States of America
PA02418

ABOUT THE AUTHOR

Jaclyn Jaycox is a children's book writer and editor. When she is not writing, Jaclyn loves drinking coffee, reading, and spending time with her family. She lives in southern Minnesota with her husband, two kids, and naughty German shepherd.

TABLE OF CONTENTS

CHAPTER 1

What Are Statements?

Tom is training his dog, Fred. Tom tells Fred to sit, and Fred sits. He tells Fred to roll over, and Fred rolls over. He then tells Fred to lie down. Fred lies down. Afterward, Tom gives Fred a treat and tells him he did a good job. Tom is using **statements** to tell Fred what to do. Statements can give commands.

Dogs follow statements from their trainers to know what to do. Computers need statements, too.

Coders use statements
to write computer code.

Computer **coders** use statements, too. Coders are people who write computer **code**. Code is a set of instructions that a computer follows. Statements are an important part of computer code. They tell a computer what actions it needs to do. Just as Fred obeys Tom's commands, a computer does what statements tell it to do. There are many different kinds of statements.

CHAPTER 2

If-Then and *If-Else* Statements

One kind of statement is an *if-then* statement. For example, if Fred sits when Tom tells him to sit, then Fred gets a treat. When writing *if-then* statements, coders must decide what the **condition** will be. A condition must be either true or false. When a condition is met, it is considered true. If the condition is true, the computer runs the code connected to the *then* part of the statement.

A dog gets a treat on the condition that it does what it is told.

Coders use if-then *statements to write the code for buttons.*

If-then statements allow people to interact with programs. Many programs and websites have buttons to click. Some buttons play songs. Others pick a level in a game or change the page. Buttons use conditions. For example, if a person pushes a play button, then a song will play. The condition is that the button must be clicked. When the button is clicked, the condition is true. The code to play the song will only run if the condition is true.

Sometimes the condition is false. In that case, a coder can write instructions that tell the computer to run a different set of code. This other code is an *if-else* statement.

If-else statements are used for passwords. The password is the condition. When someone enters a password, the program checks to see if the password is correct. If it is correct, then the condition is true. The computer then runs code that lets the person into the program. If the password is incorrect, the condition is false. Then the code connected to the *if-else* statement runs. This code locks the user out.

```
 if (condition_is_true) {
       run_this_code
 } else {
       run_this_other_code
 }
```

Here is an example of an *if-else* statement. The *if* marks the beginning of the statement. The condition goes in parentheses. The code the computer follows if the condition is true goes in curly braces. Underneath is the *else*. The *else* marks the code the computer follows if the condition is false. That code also goes in curly braces.

CHAPTER 3

For and *While* Statements

Another type of statement is a *for* statement. A *for* statement tells a computer to repeat an action a set number of times. This type of statement is used in **loops**. Loops are a type of code. They tell a computer to repeat an action.

Suppose a coder uses a *for* statement to make a computer repeat a song three times. Each time the song repeats, the computer checks to see if the song has played three times. Once the song has played three times, the computer stops playing the song.

A for *statement* can make a song repeat a certain number of times.

For statements are helpful when coders know how many times an action needs to be repeated. If coders do not know how many times to have an action repeat, they can use *while* statements. *While* statements have conditions. A *while* statement tells a computer to repeat an action as long as the condition is true. Once the condition is false, the computer stops the action.

```
while (condition_is_true) {
        run_this_code
}
```

Here is an example of a *while* statement. The *while* marks the beginning of the statement. The condition goes between parentheses. The code for the computer to follow if the condition is true goes between curly braces.

Statements are an important part of making computers work.

A coder could use *while* statements to make a computer play a list of songs. The computer would play songs as long as there are songs left to play. Once the computer has played all of the songs, it stops playing music.

If-then, *if-else*, *for*, and *while* statements are just a few types of statements in code. Computer code is made up of many different statements that do different things. Without statements, computers would not be able to do all the amazing things they do today.

Q: What can statements give?

    a. commands

    b. loops

    c. actions

    d. none of the above

A: a. commands

Q: What is a condition?

A: A condition is something that is needed before a set of code can run.

Q: What type of statement makes a computer repeat an action?

    a. *if-else* statement

    b. *for* statement

    c. *while* statement

    d. both b and c

A: d. both b and c

Q: What is something that *if-then* statements are used for?

A: *If-then* statements are used for coding buttons.

GLOSSARY

code (KOHD) Code is a list of instructions that computers follow to do things. The computer follows code that makes it play a song three times.

coders (KOHD-urz) Coders are people who write code. Coders use *if-then* statements.

condition (kun-DISH-uhn) A condition is something that is needed before a set of code can run. A correct password is a condition that must be true.

loops (LOOPS) Loops are a type of code that tells a computer to repeat an action. The loop told the computer to play a song on repeat.

statements (STAYT-muhnts) Statements are things that are said, and in code they give computers commands. *For* statements tell computers to repeat actions.

IN THE LIBRARY

Harris, Patricia. *Understanding Coding Using Conditionals.*
New York, NY: PowerKids Press, 2017.

Scott, Marc. *A Beginner's Guide to Coding.*
New York, NY: Bloomsbury, 2017.

Wood, Kevin. *Get Coding with Logic.*
New York, NY: Rosen Publishing, 2018.

ON THE WEB

Visit our website for links about coding:
childsworld.com/links

Note to Parents, Teachers, and Librarians: We routinely verify our
Web links to make sure they are safe and active sites.
So encourage your readers to check them out!

INDEX